STEVE PARISH

PHOTOGRAPHING AUSTRALIA'S
LANDSCAPES

INTRODUCTION

Photographing Australia's Landscapes has been created in the hope that it will inspire and assist you to make your own images of some of the most spectacular landforms in the world.

I have discovered that in many ways photographing landscapes requires more patience than photographing wildlife. It certainly requires the photographer to make more conscious decisions. When an animal pops up in front of the lens, there is little choice but to take the picture. Landscapes, on the other hand, demand careful planning and lots of patience. Take a photograph of even a spectacular feature at the wrong time of day, when the light is high and harsh, and the results may be stark and unappealing. Wait until the sun is low in the sky, enriching the colours of the scene, and the photograph could be a masterpiece.

The "look" of any photograph depends on how long the film was exposed to the image of the subject through a particular type of lens. I like to think that the photographer can add something unique – call it soul – to the technological effects. I aim to use the tools of photography to interpret my vision and to produce a picture which makes the viewer react emotionally to the subject. I've heard this spontaneous response called the "WOW!" reaction. If you, the reader, have had that "WOW!" feeling from time to time when looking through *Photographing Australia's Landscapes*, I am amply rewarded for the fourteen years that went into the making of the pictures in its pages.

The photographs in this book show a selection of the landscapes generally considered to be Australia's most dramatic, following a sequence you would see if travelling around the continent clockwise, beginning at Cape York. They were all taken between 1981 and 1995, on Nikon 35mm cameras (the two underwater shots were taken on a Nikon underwater camera). The Nikkor lenses used included wide-angles (with focal lengths between 15mm and 35mm), lenses of medium focal lengths (from 50mm to 105mm) and tele-lenses ranging from 200mm to the magnificent 600mm. An 80-200mm zoom lens proved a most versatile addition to the outfit. The film used was Kodachrome or Ektachrome, with an ASA rating of either 64 or 100.

Australia is a marvellous place to live, and a wonderful continent to photograph. I hope this book inspires those of you who are not already photographers to join me in recording its beauty.

Steve Parish

ULURU, ULURU NATIONAL PARK, NORTHERN TERRITORY
Nikon, 80-200mm, 1/250th sec, f8, Kodachrome 64

PREVIOUS PAGES:

AUSTRALIAN ALPS, VICTORIA
Nikon, 24mm, 1/250th sec, f5.6, Kodachrome 64

BOABS, MEDA STATION FLOODPLAIN, THE KIMBERLEY
Nikon, 80-200mm, 1/60th sec, f4, Kodachrome 64

CHILLAGOE-MUNGANA CAVES NATIONAL PARK, QUEENSLAND
Nikon, 600mm IFED, 1/30th sec, f5.6, Kodachrome 64

EXPLORING NEAR THE MURRAY RIVER, NEW SOUTH WALES
Nikon, 80-200mm, 1/125th sec, f8, Kodachrome 64

ACCEPT
THE CHALLENGE

We can all dream of far places and of the marvellous photographs we could take if, by lucky chance, we could travel to those places. Dreaming is fine, but turning dreams into reality is a challenge that can change your life.

The secret formula for achievement is to learn your photographic skills before you ever set out on your journeys of discovery. While you plan your adventures, you can learn about lenses, films and exposures in the course of taking pictures of trees, hills and beaches near your home. When you finally find magnificent forests, rugged mountains and spectacular coasts in front of your lens, you will have learned your trade and can confidently tackle the task of capturing them on film.

When the hands which work the camera perform their task automatically, the heart and soul of the photographer are freed to create masterpieces.

VIEW FROM THE HORN, MOUNT BUFFALO, ALPINE NATIONAL PARK, VICTORIA
Nikon, 15mm, 1/60th sec, f5.6, Ektachrome 64

AERIAL VIEW, JARDINE RIVER NATIONAL PARK, QUEENSLAND
Nikon, 35mm, 1/500th sec, f2.8, Ektachrome 100

AERIAL VIEW, DUNE SYSTEM NEAR SHELBURNE BAY, CAPE YORK, QUEENSLAND
Nikon, 15mm, 1/500th sec, f5.6, Ektachrome 64

Queensland's Cape York covers an enormous area and includes just about every imaginable type of Australian landscape, from grassy plains to mountain rainforests to coastal sand-dunes. Ground travel is often made difficult by poor roads and is virtually impossible during the Wet. However, I find that while aerial photography allows the production of spectacular images, taking time to travel the Cape in a four-wheel-drive can lead to pictures which are just as exciting because of their intimacy and eye-witness impact.

TERMITE MOUNDS, LAKEFIELD NATIONAL PARK, QUEENSLAND
Nikon, 15mm, 1/125th sec, f16, Kodachrome 64

PENTECOST ISLAND, WHITSUNDAY NATIONAL PARK, QUEENSLAND
Nikon, 80-200mm, 1/1000th sec, f5.6, Ektachrome 100

Queensland's Whitsunday Islands are splendid in their scenic diversity. They also offer untold opportunities for relaxation – and photography. The sea-eagle's viewpoint gives real appreciation of the splendours of continental islands such as those in the Whitsunday Group, which when photographed at water-level become fragmented into harbours and forested sea-slopes. Use of an 80-200mm lens allowed me to choose whether to photograph all of Pentecost Island, as shown above, or to zoom in to isolate some scenic feature. A co-operative pilot positioned the aircraft so I could use a wide-angle lens to capture the snowy sweep of Whitehaven Beach in brilliant focus.

WHITEHAVEN BEACH, WHITSUNDAY NATIONAL PARK, QUEENSLAND
Nikon, 35mm, 1/1000th sec, f5.6, Ektachrome 100

FOLLOWING PAGES: HILL INLET, WHITSUNDAY NATIONAL PARK, QUEENSLAND
Nikon, 35mm, 1/500th sec, f5.6, Ektachrome 100

North Queensland offers some of the world's most beautiful rainforest scenes, but it is often difficult to find a viewpoint from which to record the forest through the trees. Rivers and creeks, which create open spaces in the forest, may offer a solution to this problem.

For this image of the Mossman River, I took a low, though rather damp and perilous viewpoint. I used a tripod to minimise camera-shake and selected a slow shutter-speed, which allowed the water to rush and foam in the picture as it does in real life. As I wanted the centre of interest to be the waterworn, sensuously rounded rocks, I spot-metered on them. This brought out their colours and contours, leaving the swirling water highlighted in brilliant white.

MOSSMAN RIVER, DAINTREE NATIONAL PARK, QUEENSLAND
Nikon, 35mm, 1/30th sec, f11, Ektachrome 64

I love the rainforest and have spent many frustrated hours trying to capture its fascination on film. The difficulties are many. The trunks of rainforest trees are tall and straight, and many interesting features, such as ferns and fungi, may grow at considerable heights. Also, the dense rainforest canopy cloaks everything beneath it in shade, making long film exposures necessary. Where a tree has fallen, the shaft of bright light which pours into the forest overpowers the surrounding dimness, and transparency film finds it difficult to cope with both sunshine and deep shadow.

Eventually, after analysing why some pictures succeeded while others failed, I made up a set of rules for myself:

- Work on a bright yet overcast day.
  This will eliminate shadows.
- Make sure there is no wind to move
  foliage during long exposures.
- Use a tripod, an open shutter and
  a cable release.

Following these rules, I have found that many of my photographs, made with ultra-long exposures, have produced images which surprised me. This is because many elements in the original scene were simply not visible to the human eye, but the long film exposure reproduced them in all their exquisite beauty.

CAPE TRIBULATION NATIONAL PARK, QUEENSLAND
Nikon, 28mm, 1/30th sec, f16, Ektachrome 100

CAPE TRIBULATION NATIONAL PARK, QUEENSLAND
Nikon, 80-200mm, 1/125th sec, f8, Kodachrome 64

The stunning area north of Cairns where tropical rainforest meets the jewel-toned waters of the Great Barrier Reef is fascinating to photograph. Here, the Great Dividing Range runs north to south and crowds the coast, so once the sun is past its zenith shadows fall fast upon the seaward slopes of the mountains. In order to show detail on land and in sea, it is necessary to schedule photography for the morning. In the afternoon, I work from the eastern or the seaward side. If conditions are right, the mountainous background is dramatically shadowed by storm clouds, while the sea, the beach and its fringing palms are still brightly illuminated.

CAPE TRIBULATION NATIONAL PARK, QUEENSLAND
Nikon, 80-200mm, 1/125th sec, f8, Kodachrome 64

FOLLOWING PAGES: COOLOOLA NATIONAL PARK, QUEENSLAND
Nikon, 80-200mm, 1/125th sec, f8, Kodachrome 64

MAGNETIC ISLAND, QUEENSLAND
Nikon, 15mm, 1/60th sec, f5.6, Kodachrome 64

When checking out the scene above, I decided that the foreground rocks added drama to an otherwise ordinary little cove. In order to get both rocks and headland sharp, I used a 15mm wide-angle lens. The picture opposite also pays tribute to the power of the wide-angle lens to produce a focus which stretches from here to seeming eternity. These images show how it is possible to create drama through emphasis on perspective and the use of light.

MAGNETIC ISLAND, QUEENSLAND
Nikon, 15mm, 1/60th sec, f16, Kodachrome 64

FOLLOWING PAGES: TOWNSVILLE TOWN COMMON
Nikon, 80-200mm, 1/125th sec, f11, Ektachrome 100

FLINDERS RIVER, PORCUPINE GORGE NATIONAL PARK, QUEENSLAND
Nikon, 24mm, 1/125th sec, f16, Kodachrome 64

In Australia's Outback, which is usually arid and often flat, mountain ranges, and the gorges which water has carved through them, are welcome places to linger and photograph. Reflections in mirror-smooth water can be even more beautiful than the rock walls they image.

LAWN HILL GORGE, LAWN HILL NATIONAL PARK, QUEENSLAND
Nikon, 15mm, 1/125th sec, f8, Kodachrome 64

In the image above, the canoes have made the water-surface tremble, shimmering the reflections it carries into iridescent beauty. Lawn Hill Gorge is one of the finest areas for bird photography in Australia, so if you visit make sure you pack any telephoto lenses you possess.

UNDERWATER SCENE, GREAT BARRIER REEF, QUEENSLAND
Nikon RS, 20-35mm, 1/60th sec, f5.6, Ektachrome 100 flash fill

AERIAL VIEW OF GREEN ISLAND, GREAT BARRIER REEF, QUEENSLAND
Nikon, 50mm, 1/500th sec, f2.8, Kodachrome 64

Above and opposite are just three of the many wonderful aspects of the awesome Great Barrier Reef which stretches up the coast of Queensland to Torres Strait. On the Reef, the photographer can indulge to the ultimate a passion for filming under the sea or on its surface. There are endless opportunities for making pictures of islands and cays, and for filling countless frames with a diversity of wondrous marine creatures. Taking to the air is one of the best ways to capture the immensity and magnificence of this unique World Heritage area.

AERIAL VIEW OF LADY MUSGRAVE ISLAND, GREAT BARRIER REEF, QUEENSLAND
Nikon, 35mm, 1/500th sec, f5.6, Ektachrome 64

AERIAL VIEW OF FITZROY ISLAND, GREAT BARRIER REEF, QUEENSLAND
Nikon, 35mm, 1/500th sec, f5.6, Ektachrome 100

AERIAL VIEW OF ERSKINE ISLAND, GREAT BARRIER REEF, QUEENSLAND
Nikon, 50mm, 1/250th sec, f4, Kodachrome 64

GLASSHOUSE MOUNTAINS ACROSS PUMICESTONE PASSAGE, BETWEEN BRIBIE ISLAND AND MAINLAND, QUEENSLAND
Nikon, 80-200mm, 1/250th sec, f11, Kodachrome 64

Shooting a dramatic sunset is always a challenge. If I can find a scene which combines western sky with water and other scenic foreground features, I set the camera on the tripod then wait for the sun to drop below the horizon. I remember to spot-meter away from the sun and I'm always aware that it is worth waiting for the afterglow, when the distraction created by the sinking fireball that is the sun has disappeared. A point of interest, such as the canoeist in the picture above, or the pelicans above right, can turn a nice sunset into a memorable one. I find waiting for light to change an enormously relaxing experience, and I do much of my most creative thinking during these solitary moments.

PELICANS, PUMICESTONE PASSAGE, QUEENSLAND
Nikon, 300mm, 1/250th sec, f8, Kodachrome 64

ELAMBA FALLS, LAMINGTON NATIONAL PARK, QUEENSLAND
Nikon, 24mm, 1/10th sec, f5.6, Ektachrome 100

When is a waterfall difficult to photograph? In Australia's north, in the Dry season, when it may be reduced to a trickle. However a photographic trip in the Wet will discover waterfalls in full glory and, using a tripod and a slow shutter speed, it is then possible to record them in all their silvery glory. A bright but overcast day, which allows some detail to be detected under overhanging rocks and foliage, will give the best photographic results.

LAMINGTON NATIONAL PARK, SOUTHEAST QUEENSLAND
Nikon, 80-200mm, 1/125th sec, f8, Kodachrome 64

I tackle rainforest photography with energy and passion, which is lucky because I usually end up backpacking in many kilos of equipment. I try to keep individual items, such as a tripod, light but, even though I will probably end up using only one lens, I like having plenty of options available. A zoom lens, such as the useful 80-200mm, may help cut down on the load and make room for something else, such as even *more* film!

Southern Queensland's offshore sand islands offer wonderful photographic opportunities. In this subtropical location, this is especially true during the months of January and February, when dramatic skies complement the splendour of beaches and dunes. Often a morning will dawn almost cloudless then, as the day progresses, storm clouds will build up in preparation for an evening thunderstorm.

The North Stradbroke beachscape shown here has three elements which counterpoint the beauty of sand and sea. First is the luminous sky with its delicate wisps of cloud. Second is the scattering of silver birds across the foreground, their purity echoing the foam-capped waves. Third is the tiny meditative figure at the far left, which adds a human element to nature's splendid stage setting.

FRASER ISLAND, QUEENSLAND
Nikon, 15mm, 1/250th sec, f11, Kodachrome 64

A photograph should invite the viewer to share the special emotional experience it represents. The calm and ethereal image above, with its dreamy reflections, contains no jarring, harsh shapes or colours. It is light-filled and serene. The action-filled coastal scene on the right portrays the continual conflict between ocean and shore. Choppy waves besiege battlements of stone, under a sky whose scudding clouds echo the attacking lines of the whitecaps below.

NORTH STRADBROKE ISLAND, QUEENSLAND
Nikon, 15mm, 1/125th sec, f8, Kodachrome 64

FINGAL BAY, PORT STEPHENS, NEW SOUTH WALES
Nikon, 105mm, 2 secs, f22, Kodachrome 64

Which is more effective in a photograph, pin-sharpness or blurred beauty? When it comes to water, either technique may be effective.

The scene on the left was shot using a shutter-speed fast enough to freeze the moment when a wave's final edge of foam retreats from the sand. The image above was made over a period of two seconds, so the breaking waves recorded lines of energy on the film. In both cases, I took an exposure-meter reading from the rocks, not from the water.

FINGAL BAY, PORT STEPHENS, NEW SOUTH WALES
Nikon, 15mm, 1/125th sec, f11, Kodachrome 64

45

BYRON BAY, NEW SOUTH WALES
Nikon, 200mm, 1/250th sec, f8, Kodachrome 64

Here are two views of Cape Byron lighthouse, which stands on the most easterly point of Australia. The first, above, is a long view which includes sea, sand, sky and reflections (the reflected cloud in the foreground neatly echoing and balancing its original above). The other image, opposite, shows the lighthouse on its headland, silhouetted against the sunrise. It has been isolated and drawn towards the viewer by the magnifying powers of a 600mm lens. Both pictures illustrate the truth that the photographer who sleeps in is missing one of the two best times of day for making pictures of landscapes and many other things as well.

BYRON BAY LIGHTHOUSE, CAPE BYRON, NEW SOUTH WALES
Nikon, 600mm, 1/250th sec, f5.6, Kodachrome 64

FOLLOWING PAGES: THE THREE SISTERS, BLUE MOUNTAINS NATIONAL PARK, NEW SOUTH WALES
Nikon, 35mm, 1/125th sec, f8, Ektachrome 64

THE BLUE MOUNTAINS, NEW SOUTH WALES
Nikon, 15mm, 1/125th sec, f8, Kodachrome 64

Some Australian landmarks, such as the famous Three Sisters which stand above the spectacular Jamison Valley in the Blue Mountains, are constantly photographed. It is a challenge to portray such scenes in a different fashion, so the person viewing the picture pauses, then looks again. In the image on the preceding pages, warm lighting isolates the Three Sisters from their scenic setting. In the picture above, the ominous sky draws attention to the rugged sandstone cliffs, while the use of a wide-angle lens allows a grass tree to offer sharply focused foreground interest. The image opposite was taken from a viewpoint which shows the Sisters as an integral part of the Jamison Valley landscape rather than as a separate feature.

THE THREE SISTERS, THE BLUE MOUNTAINS, NEW SOUTH WALES
Nikon, 300mm, 1/125th sec, f11, Kodachrome 64

WENTWORTH FALLS, THE BLUE MOUNTAINS, NEW SOUTH WALES
Nikon, 35mm, 1/8th sec, f22, Kodachrome 64

If I am going to photograph a waterfall, I hope for an overcast day. I even appreciate the charm of mist, which veils waterfall and stream in swirling mystery. Viewing these images, I remember that a photographer should always be alive to the possibilities of a landscape and look beyond the obvious subject. The delightful filmy cascade above right is just below the falls shown above. The same water flows over it, but its atmosphere and appeal are all its own. The photograph above also reminds me that I should always check my film supply before I descend hundreds of steps. When I reached this site I opened my bag to find I had only two frames left. Ah! Sweet exercise!

WENTWORTH FALLS, THE BLUE MOUNTAINS, NEW SOUTH WALES
Nikon, 24mm, 1/15th sec, f11, Kodachrome 64

FOLLOWING PAGES: AERIAL VIEW, KOSCIUSKO NATIONAL PARK, NEW SOUTH WALES
Nikon, 35mm, 1/500th sec, f2.8, Kodachrome 64

MOUNT BOGONG, ALPINE NATIONAL PARK, VICTORIA
Nikon, 600mm, 1/125th sec, f5.6, Kodachrome 64

The Australian Alps, in southeastern New South Wales and northeastern Victoria, are a photographer's wonderland in winter. Just remember to wear warm clothing, and gloves or mittens, to keep your fingers supple enough to reload film and to deal with other technicalities.

Colour film is capable of capturing all the subtleties and nuances of snow, but finds it difficult to render its brilliance while at the same time showing rocks, leaves and sky in their natural colours. When taking snow-scenes, I have found it best to meter on greenery or sky. A picture exposed for snow will show too-dark sky and trees. Enchanting snow-scenes can be taken at dawn and dusk.

KOSCIUSKO NATIONAL PARK, NEW SOUTH WALES
Nikon, 15mm, 1/250th sec, f11, Ektachrome 64

KOSCIUSKO NATIONAL PARK, NEW SOUTH WALES
Nikon, 35mm, 1/500th sec, f5.6, Kodachrome 64

KOSCIUSKO NATIONAL PARK, NEW SOUTH WALES
Nikon, 24mm, 1/250th sec, f5.6, Kodachrome 64

The rocks, gorges and forests of the Warrumbungles offer endless opportunities for picture-making, but, like many of Australia's most scenic places, some of their best aspects are difficult to reach in a vehicle.

I don't enjoy trudging up mountain tracks carrying heavy equipment, so I try to keep my gear light, but I have learned through bitter experience that the lens I need is always the one I left back at base camp, so I tend to take the lot. This is one situation where the versatile zoom lens comes into its own, as it offers a variety of focal lengths in one piece of apparatus.

On long treks, I carry my cameras and lenses in a backpack, which allows my arms freedom to haul me up steep parts of a track, or to carry a camera for opportunistic picture-taking. There is nothing more frustrating than spotting a Wedgetailed Eagle sitting in all its majesty on a high branch overlooking a valley and realising that by the time the camera has been hauled from its hiding place and the lens cap removed the bird will have flown!

WARRUMBUNGLES NATIONAL PARK, NEW SOUTH WALES
Nikon, 24mm, 1/125th sec, f8, Kodachrome 64

UNDERWATER VIEW OF KELP, BASS STRAIT, AUSTRALIA
Nikon RS, 15mm, 1/60th sec, f5.6, Kodachrome 64

There are times when I am sure I am half-seal, for I am utterly happy when beneath the sea with my camera. The Southern Ocean has its own problems, including very cold water and rapid loss of light with depth, but modern diving and photographic gear provide some solutions and the underwater cathedrals of the kelp forests never fail to fill me with awe.

WILSONS PROMONTORY, VICTORIA
Nikon, 600mm, 1/125th sec, f5.6, Kodachrome 64

Australia's southern coast offers many picturesque granite headlands. I try to use another promontory as a vantage point, so the coast unfolds behind my subject and gives depth and perspective to the image. A place such as Wilsons Promontory offers other scenic delights, including isolated beaches, heathlands, wildlife and, in springtime, a visual feast of wonderful wildflowers.

BEAUCHAMP FALLS, OTWAY RANGES, VICTORIA
Nikon, 35mm, 1/10th sec, f8, Kodachrome 64

There are places in Australia which are just crammed with wonderful subjects for photographs. An outstanding example of these marvellous places is the area of Victoria's southern coastline accessible from the Great Ocean Road, which includes the Otway Ranges. The cool temperate rainforests of the ranges, with their ferny gorges and silver-veil waterfalls, offer countless opportunities for image-making, especially if the photographer is willing to walk a little. In these shady places, a slow shutter speed will ensure great depth of field, like that in the picture opposite, as well as showing movement in the tumbling water.

HOPETOUN FALLS, OTWAY RANGES, VICTORIA
Nikon, 15mm, 1/10th sec, f11, Kodachrome 64

FOLLOWING PAGES: THE TWELVE APOSTLES, PORT CAMPBELL NATIONAL PARK, VICTORIA
Nikon, 80-200mm, 1/60th sec, f11, Ektachrome 64

THE TWELVE APOSTLES, PORT CAMPBELL NATIONAL PARK, VICTORIA
Nikon, 600mm, 1/250th sec, f5.6, Kodachrome 64

It is easy enough to put a picture of the famous Twelve Apostles on film. The achievement is to capture the grandeur and loneliness of their gallant, last-ditch stand against the hungry ocean.

I like to set my camera up late in the afternoon, then outwait the pillars' other snap-happy admirers. Eventually my rivals will all have gone and I can let the love-affair between these gallant survivors and my camera run its course. Then, if I am lucky, I can watch as the last light fades and Little Penguins begin to emerge like tiny soldiers from the waves.

ONE OF THE TWELVE APOSTLES, PORT CAMPBELL NATIONAL PARK, VICTORIA
Nikon, 80-200mm, 1/60th sec, f11, Kodachrome 64

MOUNT ARAPILES, VICTORIA
Nikon, 15mm, 1/125th sec, f11, Kodachrome 64

Think of a photograph as a painting. When the painting is complete, it is framed. A photograph can be framed while it is being created – just use a wide-angle lens so that the framing element, such as the pinetrees in the picture of well-known rockclimbing playground Mount Arapiles above, is in focus. The Grampians waterfall opposite is partly framed by a "windowsill" of foreground rocks, whose shape is echoed by the rainbow above.

MCKENZIE FALLS, THE GRAMPIANS NATIONAL PARK, VICTORIA
Nikon, 35mm, 1 sec, f22, Kodachrome 64

CRADLE MOUNTAIN-LAKE ST CLAIR NATIONAL PARK, TASMANIA
Nikon, 600mm, 1/125th sec, f5.6, Ektachrome 100

I have learned never to say to myself, "This scene will still be there tomorrow – I'll come back and photograph it then!" The scene will certainly be there, but no-one can guarantee that the weather will favour filming.

In Tasmania's marvellous mountains the sky is overcast during nine months of the year, and I arrived at Cradle Mountain-Lake St Clair National Park on the first clear day in two months. I was tired, but the scenery was so superb that my lust to make pictures won out and I hauled out the camera. The following day, when the heaths and mountains had hidden behind grey mists, I was glad that passion had overruled mere exhaustion.

LAKE DOVE, CRADLE MOUNTAIN-LAKE ST CLAIR NATIONAL PARK, TASMANIA
Nikon, 15mm, 1/30th sec, f22, Ektachrome 400

AERIAL VIEW OF AUSTRALIA'S MOST SOUTHERLY POINT, SOUTH EAST CAPE, TASMANIA
Nikon, 35mm, 1/500th sec, f5.6, Kodachrome 64

AERIAL VIEW OF STEPHENS BAY, SOUTH WEST NATIONAL PARK, TASMANIA
Nikon, 35mm, 1/500th sec, f5.6, Kodachrome 64

Picture-taking from a small plane controlled by a sympathetic pilot is like riding a magic carpet, which swoops low over Nature's wonders at your command. Tasmania's southern coastline has a sheer splendour that ranks it high on my list of Australia's most scenic landscapes. When the plane finally turned for base after I had photographed its capes and bays, I clutched the bag of exposed films and felt like Sinbad the Sailor returning from a voyage with a cargo of treasure.

AERIAL VIEW OF PRECIPITOUS BLUFF, SOUTH WEST NATIONAL PARK, TASMANIA
Nikon, 105mm, 1/500th sec, f5.6, Kodachrome 64

Generally speaking, the closer a pilot is willing to take his aircraft to the landscape feature I wish to photograph the better. We usually find it necessary to compromise between my desire to skim mountain peaks and zoom through gorges and the pilot's understandable concern for his machine (and our lives). I have found that a helicopter, particularly one large enough to transmit a minimum of vibration from the rotors, is preferable to a plane as a photographic platform.

AERIAL VIEW OF ARTHUR RANGE, SOUTH WEST NATIONAL PARK, TASMANIA
Nikon, 35mm, 1/250th sec, f11, Ektachrome 100

FOLLOWING PAGES: ALAME WOODLANDS, MOUNT FIELD NATIONAL PARK, TASMANIA
Nikon, 15mm, 1/60th sec, f8, Kodachrome 64

AERIAL VIEW OF THE RIVER MURRAY, SOUTH AUSTRALIA
Nikon, 50mm, 1/500th sec, f8, Kodachrome 64

These two views of the Murray River floodplain early in the morning show the differences in atmosphere possible in a close-up photo and a long shot which are taken in much the same location but from two utterly different perspectives. In these two images, early morning sun, massive river gums and the mist that rises at the interface of warmer water and cooler air create visual magic.

RIVER RED GUMS ON MURRAY RIVER FLATS, VICTORIA
Nikon, 80-200mm, 1/125th sec, f16, Ektachrome 64

ADMIRALS ARCH, CAPE DU COUEDIC, KANGAROO ISLAND, SOUTH AUSTRALIA
Nikon, 35mm, 1/60th sec, f5.6, Ektachrome 100

In the picture above, the lowering portal of Admirals Arch forms a natural frame for the seascape beyond. Taking the scene with a wide-angle lens ensured all elements would be in focus. I took an exposure-meter reading on the rocks of the cave floor. This exposed them correctly, but allowed the shadowed arch to go black, intensifying its dramatic effect.

Opposite is another spectacular Kangaroo Island scene, taken, like most of my landscape photos, using a tripod. Again, the exposure was metered on the foreground rocks, to capture their golden glints, which are echoed in the molten gold of the sea.

COASTLINE, KANGAROO ISLAND, SOUTH AUSTRALIA
Nikon, 15mm, 1/125th sec, f8, Ektachrome 100

REMARKABLE ROCKS, FLINDERS CHASE NATIONAL PARK,
KANGAROO ISLAND, SOUTH AUSTRALIA
Nikon, 15mm, 1/125th sec, f11, Ektachrome 100

REMARKABLE ROCKS, FLINDERS CHASE NATIONAL PARK, KANGAROO ISLAND, SOUTH AUSTRALIA
Nikon, 15mm, 1/125th sec, f11, Ektachrome 100

A "landscape" does not necessarily consist of a grand scenic sweep. It can be narrowed to one or two elements, like the stark works of the master sculptor Nature shown here, the Remarkable Rocks of Kirkpatrick Point, Kangaroo Island. I prowled around them with my wide-angle lens, assessing angles, and eventually took the giant weather-worn boulders against the sky, looking like the fossilised skulls of enormous prehistoric eagles. The human figure in the picture above gives some idea of the boulders' size.

FOLLOWING PAGES: FLINDERS RANGES NATIONAL PARK, SOUTH AUSTRALIA
Nikon, 15mm, 1/125th sec, f8, Ektachrome 64

FLINDERS RANGES, FLINDERS RANGES NATIONAL PARK, SOUTH AUSTRALIA
Nikon, 200mm, 1/125th sec, f11, Kodachrome 64

Like most Australian landscapes, South Australia's rugged Flinders Ranges are best photographed early in the morning and late in the afternoon. It is not necessary to wait until you are actually in the foothills to begin taking pictures. The ranges rise from the plains in stark glory and their ever-changing colours can be recorded framed in trees, or seen over golden grassland, or both.

FLINDERS RANGES, FLINDERS RANGES NATIONAL PARK, SOUTH AUSTRALIA
Nikon, 80-200mm, 1/125th sec, f8, Ektachrome 100

RAINSTORM OVER FLINDERS RANGES, FLINDERS RANGES NATIONAL PARK, SOUTH AUSTRALIA
Nikon, 600mm, 1/125th sec, f11, Kodachrome 64

The telephoto lens is often thought of as a tool restricted to wildlife and sports photographers, who need to drag faraway action close-up. However, it also has an important place in the landscape photographer's box of tricks. The picture above shows a rainstorm blessing a jagged Flinders Ranges skyline which has been isolated by a 600mm lens. I made sure I used a tripod to hold this superb, but weighty, piece of equipment steady.

FLINDERS RANGES, SOUTH AUSTRALIA
Nikon, 80-200mm, 1/250th sec, f11, Ektachrome 100

If you are a stranger to an area, it may take a fair amount of scouting to discover where to photograph. Once you have found your subject, you need to allow time to find out when the light on the scene will be best. A shot like the one above, which shows a not-often-seen view of the Flinders Ranges over red sand dunes, required a day's driving to discover and a long walk from the main Hawker to Leigh Creek road to record on film.

91

It is easy to think of "landscapes" as requiring mountains, trees or some other upstanding element of interest. However, the vertically disadvantaged landscape can be just as spectacular as any other. The Nullarbor Plain and the remainder of the flat country bordering Australia's Great Australian Bight offer endless opportunities for picture-making. Here, the surface of a salt-lake, drying after rare rain, has cracked into a moonscape of brine-filled shallow ponds. Low viewpoint, wide-angle lens, long shutter-speed and lens aperture shut down to f11 allowed considerable depth of focus.

CRACKING SALT CRUST ON LAKE MACDONNELL,
GREAT AUSTRALIAN BIGHT, SOUTH AUSTRALIA
Nikon, 15mm, 1/60th sec, f11, Kodachrome 64

SAND DUNE SYSTEM, FITZGERALD RIVER NATIONAL PARK, WESTERN AUSTRALIA
Nikon, 80-200mm, 1/125th sec, f8, Kodachrome 64

As of March, 1995, Australia's World Heritage Listed areas included only one place in Western Australia, Shark Bay. I like to think that one day, among other Westralian gems, the magnificent coastal dunes, sandplains and heathlands of the Fitzgerald River National Park, 240 kilometres west of Esperance, will be universally appreciated as one of the world's great wilderness areas.

SPRINGTIME, STIRLING RANGES NATIONAL PARK, WESTERN AUSTRALIA
Nikon, 35mm, 1/125th sec, f8, Ektachrome 100

In landscape photography, timing is all-important. I plan a field-trip so I reach a place at the optimal time of year for picture-making, then plan each day so I photograph when the light is best. The Stirling Ranges, near Albany, are a spectacular range that rises abruptly from the surrounding downs. In springtime, and early summer, they blaze into brilliance under carpets of wildflowers.

CAPE ARID NATIONAL PARK, WESTERN AUSTRALIA
Nikon, 15mm, 1/125th sec, f8, Kodachrome 64

A wide-angle lens should be part of every landscape photographer's armoury. These two pictures show the advantages of the vast depth of field such a lens allows. They also show the delights of photographing rocks. At left, scattered boulders contrast in texture and tone with the wind-wrinkled sand which embraces them. Above, rocks fill the foreground of the picture, eventually leading the eye to the faraway sea, with its tiny exclamation point of an island counter-balancing the massive boulder perched at centre left.

SUNRISE, CAPE ARID NATIONAL PARK, WESTERN AUSTRALIA
Nikon, 15mm, 1/125th sec, f8, Kodachrome 64

TWO PEOPLES BAY, NEAR ALBANY, WESTERN AUSTRALIA
Nikon, 15mm, 1/125th sec, f8, Ektachrome 100

These two pictures express the drama of Australia's southern coastline. The seacliffs at left, with their granite walls standing sheer against the battering sea, symbolise a harsh environment, which still threatens to engulf unwary fishermen and would annihilate any small craft foolish enough to venture too close. The photo above shows a beautiful cove which was named when "two peoples", the French and the English, were mapping Australia's coasts. In the windswept heathland behind this bay, two remarkable "re-discoveries" of creatures unseen for many years, the Noisy Scrub-bird and Gilbert's Potoroo, were made.

SEA CLIFFS NEAR ALBANY, WESTERN AUSTRALIA
Nikon, 80-200mm, 1/250th sec, f8, Kodachrome 64

THE PINNACLES, NAMBUNG NATIONAL PARK, WESTERN AUSTRALIA
Nikon, 15mm, 1/125th sec, f8, Kodachrome 64

I never forget that even on flat country I have a choice of vantage points for my camera. My first option is to crank the tripod up and take the scene from eye-level (a height of around 180 centimetres). The second is to get down on my knees, clamp the camera onto the tripod leg and work from near ground-level.

In these two pictures of the Pinnacles, viewpoint plays an important part. The image above was made at eye-level, the one on the right from a much lower angle. Colour is also important: the cloud-strewn blue sky contrasts strongly with stone pillars warmed to umber and gold by late-afternoon sun. Finally, the moving patterns formed by the clouds counterpoint the stark forms and immobility of the limestone pillars.

THE PINNACLES, NAMBUNG NATIONAL PARK, WESTERN AUSTRALIA
Nikon, 15mm, 1/60th sec, f11, Kodachrome 64

NATURES WINDOW, MURCHISON RIVER, KALBARRI NATIONAL PARK, WESTERN AUSTRALIA
Nikon, 15mm, 1/125th sec, f8, Kodachrome 64

Above is a portrait of the sandstone landmark called Natures Window. It shows the arch as a monumental feature, whose timelessness is emphasised by the ephemeral clouds rushing overhead. The close-up of the Window on the right was taken with the same 15mm lens, using the arch as a frame for the scene beyond. The viewpoint has shifted only a few metres forward, but the difference in emotional impact is enormous. Looking at the first image, the viewer remains a modern, civilised person dispassionately appreciating a landscape feature. The second image invites the viewer to imagine the feelings of prehistoric humans, looking out of the safety of their home cave, searching for potential prey and possible enemies on the plains below.

FOLLOWING PAGES: HAMERSLEY RANGE NATIONAL PARK, WESTERN AUSTRALIA
Nikon, 400 mm, 1/125th sec, f8, Kodachrome 64

VIEW THROUGH NATURES WINDOW, MURCHISON RIVER, KALBARRI NATIONAL PARK, WESTERN AUSTRALIA
Nikon, 15mm, 1/125th sec, f11, Kodachrome 64

WEANO GORGE, HAMERSLEY RANGE, KARIJINI NATIONAL PARK, WESTERN AUSTRALIA
Nikon, 15mm, 1/30th sec, f8, Kodachrome 64

Some of the continent's most fantastic arid landscapes exist in the Pilbara, on the Great Plateau of ancient rocks which makes up Australia's northwest corner. Here are spinifex-dotted plains, and ranges of subtle and glowing colours, hiding gorges in which can be found pools fringed with greenery which harbours birds and other wildlife. The fact that many views can be photographed from the roadside adds to the attractions of this area.

TWILIGHT ON THE HAMERSLEY RANGE, KARIJINI NATIONAL PARK, WESTERN AUSTRALIA
Nikon, 600 mm, 1/125th sec, f5.6, Kodachrome 64

HAMERSLEY RANGE, KARIJINI NATIONAL PARK, WESTERN AUSTRALIA
Nikon, 15mm, 1/125th sec, f8, Kodachrome 64

HAMERSLEY RANGE, KARIJINI NATIONAL PARK, WESTERN AUSTRALIA
Nikon, 15mm, 1/125th sec, f8, Kodachrome 64

JASPER OUTCROP NEAR MARBLE BAR, THE PILBARA, WESTERN AUSTRALIA
Nikon, 15mm, 1/60th sec, f16, Kodachrome 64

In the image above, the knobby texture and unusual, swirling patterns of the jasper outcrop in the foreground leads the eye to the smooth water, reflection and rugged hill behind. In the beachscape opposite, the foreground, with its variety of textures and tones, leads to the tidal flats beyond. Would the picture be as effective without the seastar?

SHELLS ON EIGHTY MILE BEACH, WESTERN AUSTRALIA
Nikon, 15mm, 1/60th sec, f8, Kodachrome 64

AERIAL VIEW OF THE FITZROY RIVER AND OSCAR RANGE, WESTERN AUSTRALIA
Nikon, 50mm, 1/500th sec, f5.6, Kodachrome 64

The Kimberley Division of far-northern Western Australia is extremely picturesque. However, travel by surface vehicle takes time and is limited in range in the Wet, while photos taken from ground-level give little idea of the vastness of the landscapes. A light aircraft transports the photographer quickly from base to subject and offers opportunities to make images such as this.

AERIAL VIEW OF THE FITZROY RIVER AND OSCAR RANGE AT GEIKIE GORGE
Nikon, 50mm, 1/500th sec, f4, Kodachrome 64

These limestone ranges, once coral reefs growing in an ancient ocean, are difficult to traverse on foot and roads through them are few. It took five minutes to travel by air from where I took the picture opposite to where I took the picture above. I enjoy photographing dramatic vistas from the usual viewpoints, but to capture a new perspective, such as shown above, is always fun.

AERIAL VIEW OF THE BUNGLE BUNGLE RANGES, PURNULULU NATIONAL PARK, WESTERN AUSTRALIA
Nikon, 50mm, 1/250th sec, f2.8, Kodachrome 64

AERIAL VIEW OF THE BUNGLE BUNGLE RANGES, PURNULULU NATIONAL PARK, WESTERN AUSTRALIA
Nikon, 50mm, 1/250th sec, f2.8, Kodachrome 64

These photographs of the marvellous banded Bungle Bungle Ranges were taken in 1983 and were amongst the first ever published.

These ranges offer many good reasons for aerial photography. The rock strata which compose the Bungle Bungles are fragile, so restrictions are placed on climbing there. They are inaccessible by road in the Wet. An aerial approach to recording them is not only convenient, but helps take pressure off one of Australia's most dramatic but also most vulnerable landscapes.

TIDAL WATERFALL, TALBOT BAY, KUNMUNYA ABORIGINAL RESERVE, THE KIMBERLEY, WESTERN AUSTRALIA
Nikon, 50mm, 1/250th sec, f5.6, Ektachrome 100

The northern Kimberley is one of the remaining great areas of wildness left on earth. One day, I will go there for an extended stay. For the present, photographs such as these serve to remind me of the area's grandeur and fascination.

TRIBUTARY, THE SAINT GEORGE BASIN, PRINCE REGENT NATURE RESERVE, THE KIMBERLEY, WESTERN AUSTRALIA
Nikon, 50mm, 1/250th sec, f5.6, Ektachrome 100

BOAB AND BOULDER, OSCAR RANGE NEAR TUNNEL CREEK, THE KIMBERLEY, WESTERN AUSTRALIA
Nikon, 15mm, 1/125th, f8, Ektachrome 64

The gouty-trunked Boab trees which are unique to the
Kimberley form the focus of many of my pictures of the
region. It seemed appropriate in this shot to balance the
massive Boab, which wears its summer crown of green
leaves, with the even more massive boulder on the slope
above it. I like the echo of the tree trunk formed by the
streaks on the boulder's side and the fact that the Boab and
the rock-pattern lean towards each other.

WINDJANA GORGE NATIONAL PARK, THE KIMBERLEY, WESTERN AUSTRALIA
Nikon, 24mm, 1/125th sec, f8, Ektachrome 64

To avoid stark contrasts between sunlight and shadow, I like to photograph gorges and valleys as near to sunset or sunrise as possible. A bit of a walk around shows me the place from which the reflections look best. Then it's just a matter of waiting until the light is right, which may even be when the sun is below the horizon. While waiting, I sit with senses on full alert, for this is the time that shy wildlife emerges from its daytime refuges to begin the night.

AERIAL PHOTO OF WATERFALLS, NORTHERN KIMBERLEY, WESTERN AUSTRALIA
Nikon, 50mm, 1/250th sec, f5.6, Ektachrome 64

Here are two photographs of waterfalls in the Kimberley, where such features may slow to a trickle in the Dry season, only to burst over their rocky ledges in exuberance when the torrential rains of the Wet arrive.

The choice of whether to take each picture in horizontal or vertical format was dictated by the span and height of the falls and the angle from which I viewed them. The sky in the vertical picture opposite sets off the red rocks above the cascades. I feel the broad expanse of dark water in the foreground of the picture above is needed to balance the brilliance of the three magnificent falls.

LENNARD RIVER GORGE, KING LEOPOLD RANGES, THE KIMBERLEY, WESTERN AUSTRALIA
Nikon, 80-200mm, 1/250th sec, f11, Ektachrome 64

FOLLOWING PAGES: BOAB TREES, DERBY, THE KIMBERLEY, WESTERN AUSTRALIA
Nikon, 400mm, 1/125th sec, f8, Ektachrome 64

POST WET SEASON FLOODPLAIN, KAKADU NATIONAL PARK, NORTHERN TERRITORY
Nikon, 80-200mm, 1/250th sec, f5.6, Ektachrome 64

In spite of heat, humidity and rain, the best time to photograph waterscapes in the Top End is during the Wet. However, the access is much easier from May to November, and the later the better if the object is photographs of birdlife concentrated on fast-disappearing water. I took the picture above from a small tin boat, oblivious to anything but the scenery, until a companion pointed out several large Saltwater Crocodiles watching us with bright-eyed interest as they floated amongst the lily-leaves nearby.

FLOODPLAIN AT PEAK OF WET SEASON, KAKADU NATIONAL PARK, NORTHERN TERRITORY
Nikon, 35mm, 1/500th sec, f8, Ektachrome 64

PREVIOUS PAGES: ANBANGBANG BILLABONG, NOURLANGIE ROCK, KAKADU NATIONAL PARK, NORTHERN TERRITORY
Nikon, 80-200mm, 1/125th sec, f8, Ektachrome 100

AERIAL VIEW OF TWIN FALLS, KAKADU NATIONAL PARK, NORTHERN TERRITORY
Nikon, 35mm, 1/500th sec, f5.6, Ektachrome 64

AERIAL VIEW OF JIM JIM FALLS, KAKADU NATIONAL PARK, NORTHERN TERRITORY
Nikon, 80-200mm, 1/30th sec, f8, Ektachrome 64

CAVERN IN ARNHEM LAND ESCARPMENT, KAKADU NATIONAL PARK, NORTHERN TERRITORY
Nikon, 15mm, 1/60th sec, f8, Ektachrome 64

BARRAMUNDI DEPICTED IN ABORIGINAL ROCK ART, KAKADU NATIONAL PARK, NORTHERN TERRITORY
Nikon, 50mm, 1/60th sec, f8, Ektachrome 64

Kakadu National Park is owned by the Aboriginal people whose ancestors have lived in the area for tens of thousands of years and the sandstone escarpment which runs through the park is a treasurehouse of Aboriginal rock art. Here, as in other areas of Australia which have traditional significance to the Aborigines, the photographer should take advice from the local people as to which places may be photographed without causing offence.

131

FLOODPLAINS AT SUNSET, KAKADU NATIONAL PARK, NORTHERN TERRITORY
Nikon, 50mm, 1/30th sec, f2.8, Ektachrome 64

Even though the sun has set on the Kakadu wetlands, there is still a fair amount of activity as birds go to roost and frogs, geckos and other nightlife become active. Just before daylight fades, a final glow lights up the sky, silhouetting trees whose mirror-images appear traced on the shining water below. This is a situation where a tripod and a slow shutter speed are essential and it is worth noting that the scene above was taken with the "standard" 50mm lens used by many photographers.

SKY DRAMA OVER THE ARNHEM LAND ESCARPMENT, NORTHERN TERRITORY
Nikon, 15mm, 1/30th sec, f5.6, Ektachrome 64

Land, sky and water are the basic elements of any landscape picture. It is easiest for the photographer to concentrate on two of these elements at a time. In the picture above, the land has been reduced to a silhouette so the sky, drifted with incandescent clouds, becomes the major feature of the photograph. I can imagine sitting in front of a photographic blow-up of this scene, feeling stress fall away as I contemplate the ancient mysteries of Arnhem Land and the advent of a new day.

WESTERN MACDONNELL RANGES NATIONAL PARK, NORTHERN TERRITORY
Nikon, 15mm, 1/125th sec, f8, Ektachrome 64

The Western MacDonnell Ranges National Park has superb scenery and is easily accessible on excellent roads. Alice Springs forms a handy base from which to explore the MacDonnell Ranges and their landscape splendours.

I am sure that colour film was invented to record the Central Australian landscape, with its red ranges, blue skies and white-trunked Ghost Gums. I always carry far more film than I think I will need and usually come home with most of the rolls exposed. When I find the right scene, I wait for the right light, then I shoot until I am sure I have covered all possibilities.

In between photo sessions, I make sure my film remains as cool as travelling circumstances allow. And I never, ever, leave film or cameras baking in a closed vehicle, or exposed to the scorching rays of the sun.

FOLLOWING PAGES: ORMISTON POUND, WESTERN MACDONNELL RANGES NATIONAL PARK
Nikon, 15mm, 1/125th sec, f8, Kodachrome 64

WALL OF GORGE, KINGS CANYON, WATARRKA NATIONAL PARK, NORTHERN TERRITORY
Nikon, 24mm, 1/125th sec, f11, Ektachrome 64

Kings Canyon is a spectacular gorge, whose walls, over 200 metres high in some places, rise high above the creek which cut its way down through the stone to create them. North of the gorge is the maze of weathered domes known as the Lost City. Opposite is the panorama of this remarkable area which can be taken from the air. Above, an intimate view of the canyon, given scale by the quietly appreciative human observer on the left.

AERIAL VIEW OF KINGS CANYON, WATARRKA NATIONAL PARK, NORTHERN TERRITORY
Nikon, 50mm, 1/500th sec, f4, Ektachrome 64

Uluru, that enormous red rock in the midst of Australia's central desert, holds many meanings for many people. It is an interesting geological phenomenon for the scientifically-minded and an object of international pilgrimage for millions who couldn't care less about the word "monolith". Most important, it is a very special place to the Aboriginal people and photography around Uluru should be done with due respect for their wishes.

At sunset, the desert around the Rock is alive with camera-carriers. I stand back, give them space to work and let the sound of motor-drives compete with the churring of crickets in the spinifex. Then, as the sun sets and the fulfilled film-takers head for dinner, I set up my tripod and settle down for a wonder-filled photographic session, all alone in the magical twilight with one of the world's greatest landscape subjects.

ULURU AT TWILIGHT, ULURU NATIONAL PARK, NORTHERN TERRITORY
Nikon, 35mm, 1/4th sec, f2.8, Ektachrome 64

FOLLOWING PAGES: ULURU FROM AFAR AND ULURU CLOSE-UP
Both images, Nikon, 15mm, 1/125th sec, f8, Ektachrome 64

The giant boulders called the Devils Marbles are strewn on the landscape about 90 kilometres south of Tennant Creek. They lie on both sides of the road and can be photographed at either sunrise or sunset with most satisfactory results.

I like to arrive at the Marbles around two hours before sunset, then take my time looking around for photographic angles. In the process, I have always discovered many other subjects for my camera, including fascinating arid-country plants, lizards, birds and other wild creatures. The Devils Marbles themselves offer many different sorts of pictorial opportunities. They may be taken in close-up, in medium shot as they lie in heaps and stacks, or taken from a distance, showing their place in the arid Central landscape.

THE DEVILS MARBLES, DEVILS MARBLES CONSERVATION RESERVE, NORTHERN TERRITORY
Nikon, 35mm, 1/10th sec, f8, Ektachrome 64

AERIAL VIEW OF KATA TJUTA, ULURU NATIONAL PARK, NORTHERN TERRITORY
Nikon, 24mm, 1/500th sec, f2.8, Ektachrome 64

The enormous rounded domes of Kata Tjuta, 32 kilometres to the west of Uluru, are stunning in their scale and their prominence in the landscape. The views opposite and above show the formations at a distance across typical Red Centre country and from the air. The domes of Kata Tjuta are of special significance to the Aboriginal people of the area and once again due respect should be paid to Aboriginal wishes when photographing them. Information on the subject can be obtained at Yulara, tourist centre for Uluru National Park.

DISTANT VIEW OF KATA TJUTA, ULURU NATIONAL PARK, NORTHERN TERRITORY
Nikon, 15mm, 1/10th sec, f8, Ektachrome 64

ITIRKAWARA (CHAMBERS PILLAR), CHAMBERS PILLAR CONSERVATION RESERVE, NORTHERN TERRITORY
Nikon, 15mm, 1/125th sec, f11, Ektachrome 64

If you want a photographic disaster, try taking colour pictures of a sandstone pillar such as Itirkawara at midday. When you look at the white-and-black result, you will wonder why you sweated in the blazing sun. Take your photos in the warm glow of sunrise or sunset and you will feel the drive of around 160 kilometres (the final 44 kilometres possible only in a 4WD) from Alice Springs was worthwhile. The first European eyes saw this fifty-metre-high column in 1860. The Aboriginal people had identified it for many thousands of years as the remains of Itirkawara, a formidable gecko ancestor.

RAINBOW VALLEY NATURE PARK, NORTHERN TERRITORY
Nikon, 80-200mm, 1/60th sec, f8, Ektachrome 100

Above is another picture taken when the sun was at a low angle, this time showing the sandstone cliffs of the James Range, just over 20 kilometres off the Stuart Highway, 75 kilometres south of "the Alice". Like Itirkawara, this landscape should not be an objective for the motorist who hates getting the vehicle dusty. I don't mind rough travel, but in the Centre I always observe a few precautions: my 4WD is in top mechanical order before I leave home and I carry essential spare parts and tools, a tow-rope and jumper leads. I take extra fuel if going off the beaten track and I always carry water, some food – and a mobile phone!

SAND DUNE, SIMPSON DESERT, NORTHERN TERRITORY/QUEENSLAND/SOUTH AUSTRALIA
Nikon, 15mm, 1/60th sec, f11, Ektachrome 64

The simple image of red dune and blue sky above bears witness that often in picture-making "less is more". It has a universal appeal, but could show any anonymous dune in any of the world's sandy deserts. The image on the opposite page is very Australian. For me, it is a sensuous landscape, whose climax is the gentle mound of the sandhill. Of course, the spinifex clumps might have tactile appeal only to those who enjoy cuddling echidnas!

SPINIFEX CLUMPS AND DUNE, SIMPSON DESERT, NORTHERN TERRITORY/QUEENSLAND/SOUTH AUSTRALIA
Nikon, 15mm, 1/60th sec, f11, Ektachrome 64

152

A PROCESS

After good rain, even the driest areas of Australia spring into life. Plants sprout leaves and buds; flowers open and produce seeds. Insects hatch and feed on the plants; reptiles, birds and mammals appear and feed on plants and insects. This is a situation for the opportunistic photographer, who, after hearing of good desert rainfall, can afford the time to climb in the car and head towards what may prove to be a picture-maker's paradise, if only a short-lived one.

The desert is a constantly changing landscape, whose aspects alter from region to region and from season to season. I find photographing this spectacular area of Australia offers never-ending challenges.

I have revisited a place after a ten-year interval, and felt as though I was seeing it for the first time. I have returned to base, viewed my "new" pictures, then pulled out the "old" ones to discover that they were totally different. This difference could be due to better film and/or camera equipment. It is more likely, however, that my "eye" for a picture, my ability to compose a shot and my ability to discover new angles from which to shoot have all developed.

The photographer, as well as the equipment, must be under a continuous process of review and improvement.

WILDFLOWERS ON DESERT DUNES
Nikon, 15mm, 1/30th sec, f8, Ektachrome 64

A COMMITMENT

As a child I constantly struggled to get adults to believe my stories about animals I had met. When in my teen years I began seeing all sorts of exciting things underwater, that need to communicate grew. All the arm-waving and talking in the world could not explain the sheer terror of confronting a White Pointer Shark alone and far from shore. I needed something that would help prove that I was not telling "fish stories". There was an answer to my need – the camera!

So I began making pictures at the age of sixteen simply to enable me to share my discoveries. My ongoing desire to make pictures was fostered by a keen interest in marine fish and I set myself the goal of photographing as many species as I could. As time progressed I found that the underwater photographic world offered amazing challenges, and I spent all my time either underwater or wishing I were. The terrestrial world, on dry land under the sky, was simply somewhere to sleep and eat between dives.

Some years later, while on a field expedition with aridland researchers in southwestern Queensland, I had my eyes opened with a jolt. I was shown landscape by experts who could unravel the mysteries of climate, soil types, geological development. They showed me how different plants associated with certain kinds of habitats and how the habitats then supported a multitude of living things. I realised that in this magic ecological cake mix there were many ingredients, and only when they were all present could the ecosystem come to life. They also showed me what a mess humans were making of Australia's often unseen landscapes.

My imagination was stirred and my compassion for the land was aroused. I became committed to showing people the marvels which existed in Australia. And so my passion for landscape photography began.

A LANDSCAPE WITHIN A LANDSCAPE, STRADBROKE ISLAND, QUEENSLAND
Nikon, 15mm, 1/60th sec, f16, Ektachrome 64

FAMOUS AUSTRALIAN LANDSCAPES

LOCATION

1	Albany	39	Karijini National Park
2	Alpine National Park	40	Kosciusko National Park
3	Arnhem Land	41	Lady Musgrave Island
4	Bass Strait	42	Lake MacDonnell
5	Blue Mountains	43	Lakefield National Park
6	Bribie Island	44	Lamington National Park
7	Byron Bay	45	Lawn Hill National Park
8	Cape Arid National Park	46	MacDonnell Ranges
9	Cape du Couedic	47	Magnetic Island
10	Cape Tribulation National Park	48	Marble Bar
11	Carnarvon Gorge	49	Mount Arapiles
12	Chambers Pillar	50	Murchison River
13	Chillagoe-Mungana Caves NP	51	Murray River
14	Cooloola National Park	52	Nambung National Park
15	Cradle Mt-Lake St Clair National Park	53	North Stradbroke Island
16	Daintree River National Park	54	Oscar Range
17	Derby	55	Otway Ranges
18	Devils Marbles	56	Pilbara
19	Eighty Mile Beach	57	Porcupine Gorge National Park
20	Erskine Island	58	Port Campbell National Park
21	Fitzgerald River National Park	59	Port Stephens
22	Fitzroy Island	60	Prince Regent River
23	Fitzroy River	61	Pumicestone Passage
24	Flinders Chase National Park	62	Purnululu National Park
25	Flinders Ranges	63	Rainbow Valley
26	Flinders Ranges National Park	64	Shelburne Bay
27	Fraser Island	65	Simpson Desert
28	Glasshouse Mountains	66	South East Cape
29	Grampians National Park	67	South West National Park
30	Great Barrier Reef	68	Stirling Ranges National Park
31	Green Island	69	Talbot Bay
32	Hamersley Range	70	Townsville
33	Jardine River National Park	71	Two Peoples Bay
34	Kakadu National Park	72	Uluru National Park
35	Kalbarri National Park	73	Warrumbungles National Park
36	Kangaroo Island	74	Watarrka National Park
37	Kimberley Division	75	Whitsunday National Park
38	King Leopold Range	76	Wilsons Promontory
		77	Windjana Gorge National Park

Steve Parish has spent his life photographing Australia.

As a boy, he had a passionate interest in wild animals. His first photographs resulted from his desire to share with others the wonders he found in South Australia's seas. A further seven years were spent recording on film the marine life of Jervis Bay, in New South Wales.
A move to Queensland inspired Steve to begin photographing the remarkable nature of Australia's north and his magnificent pictures soon attracted wide attention. In the years since, he has travelled the length and breadth of Australia, adding to his library of unique photographs of the land, its people and its wild creatures.

Steve Parish Publishing Pty Ltd was set up by Steve, and his wife and partner Jan, to publish and distribute works which would bring Australia to the world.

Through Steve's and Jan's work, millions have already discovered Australia - this book is another step on the great journey.

OTHER TITLES IN THE STEVE PARISH PUBLISHING PHOTOGRAPHING AUSTRALIA BOOK SERIES

PRODUCTION DETAILS

Photography - Steve Parish
Editing - Pat Slater, Steve Parish Publishing
Artwork - Holly Bambridge, Steve Parish Publishing
Printed in Australia - Fergies
Binding - Podlich Enterprises

First published in Australia by Steve Parish Publishing Pty Ltd
PO Box 2160 Fortitude Valley BC Queensland 4006
© Copyright photography and text
Steve Parish Publishing Pty Ltd, 1995

National Library of Australia cataloguing in publication data:
Parish, Steve - Australian Landscapes
ISBN 1 875932 07 0
1. Photography - Australia
2. Title - Photographing Australian Landscapes